Dear Parents and Educators,

Welcome to Penguin Young Readers! As parents and educators, you know that each child develops at his or her own pace—in terms of speech, critical thinking, and, of course, reading. Penguin Young Readers recognizes this fact. As a result, each Penguin Young Readers book is assigned a traditional easy-to-read level (1–4) as well as a Guided Reading Level (A–P). Both of these systems will help you choose the right book for your child. Please refer to the back of each book for specific leveling information. Penguin Young Readers features esteemed authors and illustrators, stories about favorite characters, fascinating nonfiction, and more!

In the Forest

LEVEL **1**

GUIDED
READING
LEVEL **A**

This book is perfect for an **Emergent Reader** who:
- can read in a left-to-right and top-to-bottom progression;
- can recognize some beginning and ending letter sounds;
- can use picture clues to help tell the story; and
- can understand the basic plot and sequence of simple stories.

Here are some **activities** you can do during and after reading this book:
- **Make Connections**: The three sections in this book name different plants, animals, and objects that are in the forest. Take a look at each section and brainstorm other things you might see there. For fun, have the child draw a picture of these objects or animals.
- **Word Repetition**: Reread the story and count how many times you come across the following words: *forest, in, grow, live, what.* On a separate sheet of paper, work with the child to write a new sentence for each word. Use the animals and objects brainstormed in the first activity in your new sentences!

Remember, sharing the love of reading with a child is the best gift you can give!

—Bonnie Bader, EdM
   Penguin Young Readers program

*Penguin Young Readers are leveled by independent reviewers applying the standards developed by Irene Fountas and Gay Su Pinnell in *Matching Books to Readers: Using Leveled Books in Guided Reading*, Heinemann, 1999.

To my dad, who showed me the beauty and serenity of being in the forest. And to the Black Hills National Forest, which never ceases to awe and inspire me—CK

Penguin Young Readers
Published by the Penguin Group
Penguin Group (USA) Inc., 375 Hudson Street, New York, New York 10014, USA
Penguin Group (Canada), 90 Eglinton Avenue East, Suite 700, Toronto, Ontario M4P 2Y3, Canada
(a division of Pearson Penguin Canada Inc.)

Penguin Books Ltd, Registered Offices: 80 Strand, London WC2R 0RL, England

Photo credits: cover: (sun) © Comstock/Thinkstock, (racoon, second tree) © iStockphoto/Thinkstock, (first tree, third tree, fourth tree, river) © Hemera/Thinkstock; cover, page 3: (fawn, flower) © iStockphoto/Thinkstock; page 5: (bears, grass) © iStockphoto/Thinkstock; pages 6–13,16–23, 26–32: (second tree) © iStockphoto/Thinkstock, (first tree, third tree, fourth tree) © Hemera/Thinkstock; page 6: (squirrels, stump) © iStockphoto/Thinkstock; page 7: (bears) © iStockphoto/Thinkstock; page 8: (moose, grass) © iStockphoto/Thinkstock; page 9: (blue jay, cardinal, robin, branches) © iStockphoto/Thinkstock; page 10: (doe, fawn) © iStockphoto/Thinkstock, (buck) © Hemera/Thinkstock; page 11: (top racoon) © iStockphoto/Thinkstock, (bottom racoon) © Hemera/Thinkstock; page 12: (monarch butterfly on left, monarch butterfly on pink flower) © Hemera/Thinkstock, (all other butterflies, orange flower) © iStockphoto/Thinkstock; page 13: (top skunk) © iStockphoto/Thinkstock, (bottom skunk) © Hemera/Thinkstock; page 15: (mushroom, pinecones, acorns) © iStockphoto/Thinkstock; page 16: (wildflowers) © iStockphoto/Thinkstock; page 17: (acorns) © iStockphoto/Thinkstock; page 18: (pinecones on branch) © Zoonar/Thinkstock, (all other pinecones) © iStockphoto/Thinkstock; page 19: (blueberries, strawberries) © iStockphoto/Thinkstock; page 20: (dark green leaves) © Brand X Pictures/Thinkstock, (light green leaves) © iStockphoto/Thinkstock; page 21: (mushrooms) © iStockphoto/Thinkstock; page 22: (nuts) © iStockphoto/Thinkstock; page 23: (top grass) © iStockphoto/Thinkstock, (bottom grass) © Hemera/Thinkstock; page 25: (nest with eggs) © iStockphoto/Thinkstock; page 26: (top beehive, bees) © iStockphoto/Thinkstock, (bottom beehive) © Hemera/Thinkstock; page 27: (rocks) © iStockphoto/Thinkstock; page 28: (roots) © Hemera/Thinkstock; page 29: (rivers) © Hemera/Thinkstock; page 30: (top nest) © iStockphoto/Thinkstock, (birds and nest) © Top Photo Group/Thinkstock; page 31: (logs) © iStockphoto/Thinkstock; page 32: (sun) © Comstock/Thinkstock.

Library of Congress Cataloging-in-Publication Data is available.

ISBN 978-0-448-46719-1 (pbk)   10 9 8 7 6 5 4 3 2 1
ISBN 978-0-448-46720-7 (hc)   10 9 8 7 6 5 4 3 2 1

In the Forest

by Alexa Andrews
illustrated by Candice Keimig
and with photographs

Penguin Young Readers
An Imprint of Penguin Group (USA) Inc.

See What Lives in the Forest

Squirrels live in the forest.

Bears live in the forest.

Moose live in the forest.

Birds live in the forest.

Deer live in the forest.

Raccoons live in the forest.

Butterflies live in the forest.

Skunks live in the forest.

See What Grows in the Forest

Flowers grow in the forest.

Acorns grow in the forest.

Pinecones grow in the forest.

Berries grow in the forest.

Leaves grow in the forest.

Mushrooms grow in the forest.

Nuts grow in the forest.

Grass grows in the forest.

See What Is
in the Forest

Beehives are in the forest.

26

Rocks are in the forest.

Roots are in the forest.

Rivers are in the forest.

Nests are in the forest.

Logs are in the forest.

Trees are in the forest.